Spelling Five
An Interactive Vocabulary & Spelling Workbook
for 9-Year-Olds.

(With Audiobook Lessons)

By

Bukky Ekine-Ogunlana

© **Copyright Bukky Ekine-Ogunlana 2022 – All rights reserved.**

The content of this book may not be reproduced, duplicated, or transmitted without direct written permission from the author or the publisher.

Under no circumstance will any blame or legal responsibility be held against the publisher, or author, for any damages, reparation, or monetary loss due to the information contained within this book. Either directly or indirectly. You are responsible for your own choices, actions, and results.

Legal Notice:

This book is copyright protected. This book is only for personal use. You cannot amend, distribute, sell, use, quote, or paraphrase any part, of the content within this book, without the author's or publisher's consent.

Disclaimer Notice:

Please note the information contained within this document is for educational and entertainment purposes only. All effort has been executed to present accurate, up-to-date, reliable, and complete information. No warranties of any kind are declared or implied. Readers acknowledge that the author is not engaging in rendering legal, financial, medical, or professional advice. The content within this book has been derived from various sources. Please consult a licensed professional before attempting any techniques outlined in this book

By reading this document, the reader agrees that under no circumstances is the author responsible for any direct or indirect losses incurred as a result of the use of the information contained within this document, including, but not limited to, errors, omissions, or inaccuracies.

Published by

TCEC Publishing

TCEC House

Table of Contents

Spelling Five 1
Dedication 5
Introduction 6

Spelling 5-1----- 7
Spelling 5-2 10
Spelling 5-3 13
Spelling 5-4 16
Spelling 5-5 19
Spelling 5-6 22
Spelling 5-7 25
Spelling 5-8 28
Spelling 5-9 31
Spelling 5.-10 34
Spelling 5.-11-------- 37
Spelling 5.-12 40
Spelling 5.-13 43
Spelling 5.-14 46
Spelling 5.-15 49
Spelling 5.-16 52
Spelling 5.-17 55
Spelling 5.-18 58
Spelling 5.-19 61
Spelling 5-20 64
Spelling 5-21------ 67
Spelling 5-22 70
Spelling 5-23 73
Spelling 5-24 76
Spelling 5-25 79
Spelling 5-26 82

Spelling 5-27 85

Spelling 5-28 88

Spelling 5-29 91

Spelling 5-30 94

Spelling 5-.3------ 97

Spelling 5-32 100

Spelling 5-33 103

Spelling 5-34 106

Conclusion **109**

Answers.. **111**

Other Books You'll Love! **145**

Facebook Community **150**

References **151**

Dedication

This book is dedicated to our three exceptional children and all the beautiful children worldwide who have passed through the T.C.E.C 6-16 years program over the years. Thank you for the opportunity to serve you and invest in your colorful and bright future.

Introduction

Here you are, ready to beat the fifth book of Spelling for Kids series. In Spelling Five, you get to learn 408 new words in total. So, it is ideal for nine-year-olds....

The method of studying remains the same.

That is, first hearing each word, then reading it in the sentence, then writing it down on your own, and finally checking its spelling.

Repeat the exercise to learn the spelling of the words thoroughly and persist in the words that you may find challenging.

Remember, no one becomes a master without practice.
So, are you ready to kick off the fifth level?
Let's go!

Spelling 5-1

1. Spell:
Lydia had the rare ---------------------------of speaking with the queen.

2. Spell:
Six and four make ------------------------ ten.

3. Spell:
He will be there, ----------------------------he may be a little bit late.

4. Spell:
They sat down at the beach to ---------------- at the sea.

5. Spell:
She had----------------------because of the pain she was having.

6. Spell:
The bus-------------------------------did not give her a ticket because she was rude.

7. Spell:
I pay ------------------------------- visits to my grandma because she is sick.

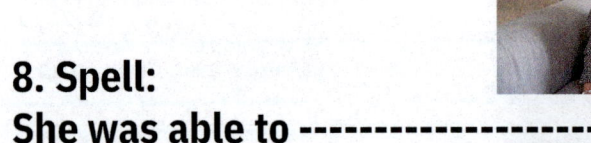

8. Spell:
She was able to ----------------------------- her teacher perfectly.

9. Spell:
She explained a different---------------------
which made more sense.

10. Spell:
The manager asked me to put a caution sign because the floor was ------------------.

11. Spell:
Noah ------------------------------ figured out his dad's password.

12. Spell:
Oliver did not ------------------------------------
the rude apology.

That's it for lesson 1. Well done!

Spelling 5-2

1. Spell:
Lisa chose to draw a -------------------------
in today's drawing lesson.

2. Spell:
Nathan put his craft on the --------------------
-------- table.

3. Spell:
He lost all his --------------------------------- in
gambling.

4. Spell:
She did not have any -----------------------
for tasty food because she was sick.

5. Spell:
In her maths book, Pricilla used ------------------------- tracing paper to enlarge and rotate a shape.

6. Spell:
My family is ------------------------------------- to me.

7. Spell:
Lilian's dad and uncle tied the ship to the ---------------------- with firm ropes.

8. Spell:
Everyone in the boy's scout admires Emmanuel for his ---------------------------------.

9. Spell:
My little sister has a great sense of ---------------------- which I also admire.

10. Spell:
The ------------------------------ sang an uplifting and inspiring song at church on Sunday.

11. Spell:
Dylan bought a broken toy, so he returned to ---------------------- a refund.

12. Spell:
The cat did ------------------------------------- Melissa's drawing.

Congrats! You have finished learning the words in lesson 2. Remember to know and understand the meaning of all the new words you have found.

Spelling 5-3

1. Spell:
The dog was buried at the pet's ---------------- last week.

2. Spell:
Will you be ------------------------ to babysit this weekend?

3. Spell:
The population of the city is, on --------------------, 100,000 people.

4. Spell:
Yusuf was put in an ----------------position with the question he picked.

5. Spell:
He got the cup at a lower price which is a real ---------------------------.

6. Spell:
Lola had a --------------------------------on her leg after the fall.

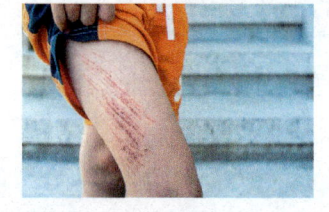

7. Spell:
The items were sorted according to their different ------------

8. Spell:
The -------------------- has twelve members who are not active.

9. Spell:
She was able to -------------------- verbally and in writing to impress the teacher.

10. Spell:
I live in a small--------------------------------with farmers.

11. Spell:
The ------------------------------ is coming up in January.

12. Spell:
Cecelia went to apologize because she had a guilty --

Great! You have finished learning the words in lesson 3.

Spelling 5-4

1. Spell:
Amy had to hold her baby brother carefully because he was still ------------------------------ after his operations.

2. Spell:
The first-floor ------------------------ is too low.

3. Spell:
Be careful with that glass because it is -----------------.

4. Spell:
The caretaker has failed to --------------------- his daily obligations.

5. Spell:
Nathan dares not to -------------------------- in Sofia's personal life.

6. Spell:
Julius lost a lot of money in a failed business ------------------that he embarked on with his friend.

7. Spell:
Lydia's mum was sick, so she got a close------------------to look after her.

8. Spell:
Kenneth will --------------------------- tomorrow if it is warm enough to go and swim.

9. Spell:
Jude came -------------------------------- in the skipping competition.

10. Spell:
In the summer, Jude and James mow their------------------ once a week.

11. Spell:
The school's playing field has an------------------------shape that is decent.

12. Spell:
The tower block has a ---------------------------- foundation.

Great! Lesson 4 is over! I suggest you get some rest before going on to the next lesson. That will help you recharge and return to the next task more refreshed! Great work!

Spelling 5-5

1. Spell:
The famous singer used -------------------with her makeup to look more glowing on stage.

2. Spell:
We grow and --------------------------------- our vegetables in our garden.

3. Spell:
Evie did not ----------------------------------- her doctor's appointment, so she got a message from the hospital.

4. Spell:
You must grab him and -------------------------- him to go through the back door.

5. Spell:
Tyler's--------------------------was wrong, but Tony's was right.

6. Spell:
The police arrived on time at the crime-----------------, which saved Eddy.

7. Spell:
Andrei and Molly made a footprint in the wet--------------.

8. Spell:
A-----------------------------------is made up of hundred years.

9. Spell:
Chloe did not--------------her sister to tidy up her room because she was running late.

10. Spell:
The------------------------decided on the case and gave his judgment.

11. Spell:
Faisal's --------------------------- salary has been increased because of his hard work and good contributions.

12. Spell:
When I go abroad, I always buy goods from -------------- stores.

Fantastic! You have finished the words in lesson 5. What a task!

Spelling 5-6

1. Spell:

"---------------------------------Gonzales" is a famous song about the fastest mouse in all of Mexico.

2. Spell:

Mrs. Smith was --------------------------------- because the classroom door was locked.

3. Spell:

It was the cleaner's--.

4. Spell:

Mr. Stanley will be ------------------------------ years old on Tuesday.

5. Spell:
Molly was told to------------------------------some cheese and spread it on the macaroni.

6. Spell:
The -------------------------- was returned to the owners after the display.

7. Spell:
Mia has a pleasant --------------------------, and hanging out with her is easy-going.

8. Spell:
Ollie tried to explain the ------------------------------- to Owen to understand better what had happened.

9. Spell:
Bailey bit his-----------------------------------, and now it is bleeding.

10. Spell:
The ---------------------------- for the school trip to France has been made today.

11. Spell:
Ethan stepped into his new----------------------------to see if they fit.

12. Spell:
-------------------------------is the best period of your life, so make the most of it and don't waste it on silly things.

Lesson 6 has come to an end. Awesome! Keep up the excellent work! And do not forget: repetition makes the master!

Spelling 5-7

1. Spell:
Carter studied pharmacy at the university to take over his mum's ---.

2. Spell:
The ------------------------ is reading quietly in the library.

3. Spell:
I see the fish --------------------------------- in the fish net.

4. Spell:
Henrietta refused to settle the ------------------------------ between her and Lainey.

5. Spell:
There was a massive--------------------------------at the back of the school today.

6. Spell:
Samuel is --------------to overtake Richard in bike riding.

7. Spell:
The--of the story is that it is natural and authentic.

8. Spell:
Kaden can -------------------------------- the science teacher perfectly.

9. Spell:
The --price was reduced by twenty percent because of the sales discount.

10. Spell:
The class stood and gave an ---------------------- to Henry for his speech.

11. Spell:
The little boy did ----------------------------------- when he was told to take his injections.

12. Spell:
My wildest dream is to travel with a ----------------------- and see the whole city from the sky.

Look how far you have gone by now. You have reached and completed lesson 7! What a student you are! Congratulations!

Spelling 5-8

1. Spell:
Danny lives on a -------------------------- road and goes to a ----------------school because her parents can afford it.

2. Spell:
The family had to ---------------------------------the court's decision because it was not favorable.

3. Spell:
The family gave us a warm ---------------- to their family home.

4. Spell:
The --------------------------------------- sat at the reception and waited for his room to be ready.

5. Spell:
Regarding her age, Emily is a --------------------------girl.

6. Spell:
Karen was able to ------------------------- a decent grade on the exam.

7. Spell:
Louie did not ---------------------------------- Nancy to his graduation.

8. Spell:
Bella sustained an ------------------------------ on her arm during the long jump she did.

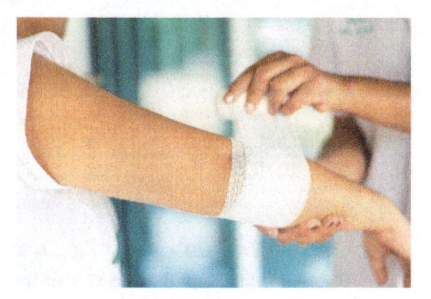

9. Spell:
Mr. Smith gave a ----------------------------------- surprise to the class after the assembly.

10. Spell:
Kayden is the only -------------------------------------- of the plane crash.

11. Spell:
The school has employed a new strict ----------------------.

12. Spell:
They played ----------------------------------- music during the musical chair.

Look at you! You are natural! And it seems that you will be a spelling bee master pretty soon! You have just finished lesson 8.

Spelling 5-9

1. Spell:
Mrs. Martins is an ----------------- and thorough teacher.

2. Spell:
I believe in God's ------------------------------ and believe that miracles can happen.

3. Spell:
The ------------------------------ he gave was persuasive.

4. Spell:
You should ask Tony about this because he is ----------- with the subject.

5. Spell:
Learning a ------------------------------ language can open doors for your career.

6. Spell:
Deb got-----------------------out of a hundred on the quiz.

7. Spell:
Martha and Mary--------------------speak on their phones.

8. Spell:
The -------------------------------- has made new laws that will affect everyone in the country.

9. Spell:
His uncle could not --------------------------------- that he would pay his rent on time.

10. Spell:
Don't -------------------------------------- the little boy for not responding to your jokes.

11. Spell:
Angela was trying to help her brother, but she found him much of a -------------------------------- than a help.

12. Spell:
Collier has lost his -- card, so he cannot go in with his class.

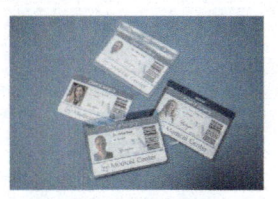

Well done! You have finished lesson 9. You should be proud of yourself! And remember this: always enunciate each word properly; this method will help you spell the word correctly.

Spelling 5-10

1. Spell:
The ---------------------- dedicated his book to his family.

2. Spell:
The new dining ---------------------------can accommodate more chairs.

3. Spell:
The new factory in town will -------------------------------- young workers so that unemployment will decrease.

4. Spell:
Tim will play football when his ------------------------ has healed.

5. Spell:
The trial will be held in the Supreme -------------------of Justice behind closed doors.

6. Spell:
The-------------------------------she had was better than the perfume Mary had bought at the shop.

7. Spell:
The ------------------- in the story was kind and humble.

8. Spell:
You must -------------------------- your goals and not get discouraged by any obstacles you meet on the way.

9. Spell:
The---------------------------number and date were not on the package.

10. Spell:
Lisa lived in the ------------------------------ after she gave birth to the twins.

11. Spell:
The ---------------------- took a while, but we got there in the end.

12. Spell:
It takes a--------------------------to be a professional in any chosen field.

You completed lesson 10 Bravo! You are doing a great job. Pretty soon, you will be an expert in spelling.

Spelling 5-11

1. Spell:
Hermione took Sophia by the ---------------------------- to cross the road.

2. Spell:
He likes to ------------------------ about his performance at the games where he won the first medal.

3. Spell:
There was no -------------------------------- that Kayden and Phoebe did any work in class today.

4. Spell:
It's my -- to live my life, so please do not interfere.

5. Spell:
The builder divided the large -------------------------- into two single rooms.

6. Spell:
He was busy; -------------, he could not attend the party.

7. Spell:
Phoebe bought a silver ---------------------- for her mum's birthday, and her mum immediately pinned it on her blouse.

8. Spell:
The class teacher was ---------------------------- with her time to help prepare the class for the final exams.

9. Spell:
Marissa wore a yellow dress which made her ------------ in the assembly.

10. Spell:
The --time for Kim to wake up is half six in the morning.

11. Spell:
Mr. Dickson was given a -------------------------------------- welcome at the palace.

12. Spell:
There are -------------------------------- bottles in the box.

You have finished the words in lesson 11. Fantastic! Don't give up! Eyes ahead to the next lesson.

Spelling 5-12

1. Spell:
The lady swept the floor and cleared the ------------------ pieces of glass.

2. Spell:
Lexi went to the ------------------------- for the first time on Friday, and most enjoyed the aerialists.

3. Spell:
Lola had to ------------------------- the music so she could hear her mum calling.

4. Spell:
The class was too ---------------------- for me to work.

5. Spell:
Car is a---------------- noun, but Toyota is a proper noun.

6. Spell:
I drank ----------------------of water after the relay race because I was thirsty.

7. Spell:
Lisa did ------------------- the loss of her dog for a long time.

8. Spell:
The carpenter has moved his shop to a new ------------- closer to the market.

9. Spell:
It takes about two weeks to get -------------------------- to join the team.

10. Spell:
Lisa behaved in a ---------------------------------- manner today in the drama class.

11. Spell:
My dad's --------------------------------is final, so we must accept and conform to it.

12. Spell:
A pleasant ---------------------------- seems to be coming from the front window to cool us down.

You have done an excellent job finishing words in lesson 12. With this rhythm, you are about to be a master in spelling soon.

Spelling 5-13

1. Spell:
After going to the gym, I always drink an ----------------- drink.

2. Spell:
You will be rewarded later for the ------------------------ you put into this project.

3. Spell:
Sophia had tomatoes and a ---------------------------------- sandwich for her lunch.

4. Spell:
The teenagers did a peaceful ---------------------------- on the field for their school rights.

5. Spell:
Staying in---helps you get in touch with your inner voice.

6. Spell:
--- in and breathe out slowly, and your panic attack will pass.

7. Spell:
She ---to apologize, but she was too proud to do it.

8. Spell:
Eating a full plate of rice did not --------------------------- him; he had to ask for more.

9. Spell:
Anderson altered the figures to ---------------------- the actual evidence to avoid getting caught.

10. Spell:
The children shouted in the studio and heard the ------- come back.

11. Spell:
Ellie-May's mum has always been her -------------------.

12. Spell:
David bought a ----------------------------------- repellent because he was going to the forest.

Congrats! You have made such Progress! You finished the words in lesson 13 already. Don't forget to practice new vocabulary every week. First, learn the meaning of the word, then the spelling of it. And then surprise everyone with your spelling skills.

Spelling 5-14

1. Spell:
Laban took ------------------------------ of Jacob and made him serve for one month without pay.

2. Spell:
The naughty boy ------------------------------ did his work when the teacher phoned his mum.

3. Spell:
The children did--their class teacher in the class.

4. Spell:
It is---------------------to walk on the path at night alone.

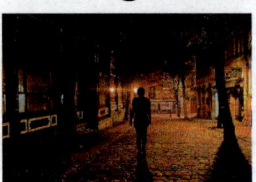

5. Spell:
The ---------------------------------- was pardoned by the Government and was set free.

6. Spell:
They were able to----------------------------------the farm without depending on rain.

7. Spell:
The show will be ---------------------------------- today from the new T.V. studio. Stay tuned!

8. Spell:
The--chapter was more interesting than this one.

9. Spell:
There is no ----------------------------------- face because beauty lies in the eyes of the beholder.

10. Spell:
George is Liam's ---.

11. Spell:
The --------------------------- has bought new laptops for the students.

12. Spell:
Her daughter did not -------------------------------------- her with the acting role she played.

What Progress! You completed lesson 14 already. You should be proud of yourself!

Spelling 5-15

1. Spell:
Our class decided to publish a school --------------------.

2. Spell:
Oscar wrote an --for the school magazine on bullying.

3. Spell:
She has formed a new ------------------------------------ of not eating in-between meals.

4. Spell:
She looks pretty in her new school-------------------------.

5. Spell:
There is a ------------------------------ to working out the nonverbal reasoning question.

6. Spell:
The ------------------------------------ of the writing was to inform the readers.

7. Spell:
We have small, --, and large size coffee; which one will you have?

8. Spell:
The ----------------------- was faulty, so we got a new one.

9. Spell:
The old lady eats tuna ----------------------------------every day for her lunch.

10. Spell:
The measurement was ---------------------------------, so you do not need to verify.

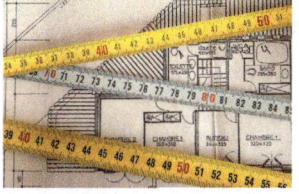

11. Spell:
The hair she is wearing is natural and ---------------------.

12. Spell:
Frankie did not believe in the carpenter's ----------------to fix the tap.

Wonderful! You have completed words in lesson 15. Keep up the great work, and remember that words matter, and most importantly, correctly written words matter.

Spelling 5-16

1. Spell:
She is at ----------------------------to stay up late because it is her school holiday.

2. Spell:
She did not ---------------------------- her expected grade because she could not be bothered to put in the effort.

3. Spell:
She turned ------------------------------------drawing into a world-class one with her painting.

4. Spell:
The --------------------------- stopped for the old lady to stroll through the zebra crossing.

5. Spell:
He did not take ------------------------------ on time, so his membership was cancelled.

6. Spell:
She gave a ------------------------------ introduction at the start of the program.

7. Spell:
Debby got an ---------------------------message when she typed the figures into the keyboard.

8. Spell:
The -- room is closed.

9. Spell:
He switched to another T.V. -------------------------------- because he was bored.

10. Spell:
He could measure the -------------------------------- of the plants with his last readings.

11. Spell:
The bank manager did not ------------------------------ the application letter.

12. Spell:
Daisy's ---------------------was leaping and running in the field.

You're almost finished with becoming a spelling master. You are doing so well! You have completed words in spelling lesson 16. Bravo!

Spelling 5-17

1. Spell:
The school ------------------------gave the Wi-Fi password to the class.

2. Spell:
Betty was leaning on her dad's ------------------------after her lunch.

3. Spell:
Lucas's------------------------------------was long and could not fit into the required space box.

4. Spell:
She was -- with her intention to help calm the baby down.

5. Spell:
She-------------------------------apologized to the caretaker for pouring water on the carpet.

6. Spell:
Harry wants to be a--------------------------------when he grows up and joins the army.

7. Spell:
Billy had a ------------------------------------ upset, so he did not have any lunch.

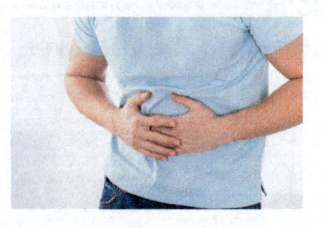

8. Spell:
Adam's boss didn't consider his job input-----------------to give him a raise.

9. Spell:
If your headache persists, I--------------------------you go to the doctor.

10. Spell:
Daniel drew a dove and painted it white as a ------------- of peace for his art homework.

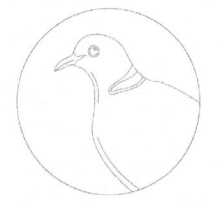

11. Spell:
The nurse came around the house to take Julia's --------

12. Spell:
Mrs. June's maths lesson helped the class to have a -------------- understanding of prime numbers.

Fantastic! You have completed spelling lesson 17!

Spelling 5-18

1. Spell:
Joshua is going to university to ----------------------------- aeronautical engineering.

2. Spell:
Sandra took the medicine spoon, leaving a-------------- taste in her mouth.

3. Spell:
Everyone was happy ------------------------------- the girl who had lost her mum.

4. Spell:
Lilian did more work because she received a lot of ---------------------------- from school.

5. Spell:
Daniel is traveling to Beijing on Sunday to see the------------------------------of China.

6. Spell:
Kate left late so she could avoid the------------------------times on the train.

7. Spell:
Oscar shared his -------------------------------with Anthony when it was raining.

8. Spell:
Lisa ordered a new set of --------------------------- for her sitting room.

9. Spell:
Ella did not get a good ------------------------------- on the comprehensive exam.

10. Spell:
Elizabeth roared like a lion to ---------------------------- Johnson, who was listening to music in his room.

11. Spell:
Lily's play materials were made of -------------------- clothes.

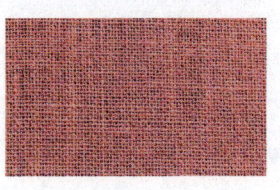

12. Spell:
Emily is Sophia's ----------------------------, the daughter of her sister.

Spelling lesson 18 is over. You finished it and, more importantly, learned the lesson's words. However, if you have doubts about one or more words, do not worry; return to the word and make as many revisions as necessary.

Spelling 5-19

1. Spell:
The ------------------------------ on the farm destroyed Mr. Elli's crops.

2. Spell:
Nick was asked to ------------------------ a candidate.

3. Spell:
With such a low salary, I----------------------to get by until the end of the month.

4. Spell:
Mr. Howard is now a member of the -------------------- of directors for the company.

5. Spell:
Lilly baked a ------------------------- steak pie for dinner.

6. Spell:
Don't -------------------------- me by telling me you will take the children away from me.

7. Spell:
Susan was ----------------------------with her handwriting when writing the competition essay.

8. Spell:
A-- of twelve is three.

9. Spell:
The teacher changed the sitting -------------------------- of everyone in the class.

10. Spell:
His eyes gleamed with -------------------------------when he opened the present.

11. Spell:
The second part of the film was ------------------------, so we were not allowed to watch it.

12. Spell:
Jude is learning his ----------------------and subtraction.

Excellent work, kid!

Spelling 5-20

1. Spell:
Nick did not ---------------------------------- that there was anything wrong with Sophie's dressing.

2. Spell:
A synonym for -- is old.

3. Spell:
The older man ---------------------------- the time his grandchildren had come to spend with him.

4. Spell:
Please don't -------------------------------- these seats, as they are intended for the elderly.

5. Spell:
Nathan will be starting -------------------- in September.

6. Spell:
All the children began to ---------------------- to hear the head boy's speech.

7. Spell:
The gardener planted a row of trees to mark the------------------of her property.

8. Spell:
The nurse wrapped a --------------------on Alfie's wound.

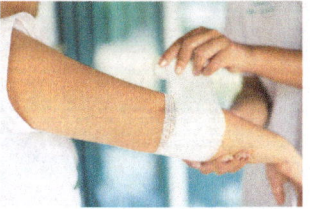

9. Spell:
Josephine's ---------------------- has made the class to be in tranquil.

10. Spell:
Jenny wears her pink satin dress only on ----------------- occasions.

11. Spell:
Charlotte bought a bar of -------------------- for her school trip.

12. Spell:
The---------------------------------Tom felt playing at the funfair was written on his face.

Great work!

Spelling 5-21

1. Spell:
The sky is ----------------------------------, and pretty soon it will rain, so take your umbrella with you.

2. Spell:
Stephan made his handwriting clear and----------------- to read.

3. Spell:
There was a piece of ----------------------------------- evidence that led to his conviction.

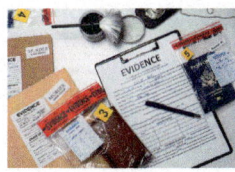

4. Spell:
The --------------------------------- will close on Tuesday.

5. Spell:
Charlie is his--------------------------------------guardian.

6. Spell:
Naomi cleaned the ---------------------------------- of the table before serving the meal.

7. Spell:
Michael has royal blood in his -------------------------------.

8. Spell:
Matilda is a --------------------------, tender, and brilliant girl, and it is a pleasure to hang out with her.

9. Spell:
Kim will ------------------------------------ the speakers at the event.

10. Spell:
A qualified tailor took the---------------------------------.

11. Spell:
Daniel had a long --------------------------- with his dad on their way to school.

12. Spell:
The teacher prepared well for the class and could------------------------all the kids.

Well done! You are nearly there.

Spelling 5-22

1. Spell:
Don't worry about me, because I will not ------------------ a thing about what happened.

2. Spell:
William had to ------------------------------------ his point with his friends.

3. Spell:
The two Congressmen will have a ------------------------ on T.V. this evening.

4. Spell:
Nancy had only a ------------------------------for breakfast.

5. Spell:
Betty's voice was not so clear and barely ------------------.

6. Spell:
Ben ate a small ----------------------------- of food because he was sick.

7. Spell:
It is---------------------------you do it on Monday or Friday.

8. Spell:
The ------------------------------------ instinct is robust even in female animals after giving birth.

9. Spell:
The new house has an ---------------------------------- pole in front of it.

10. Spell:
Leah rested her baby on her --------------------------------.

11. Spell:
Billy was very ---------------------------------------at the movie, so he closed his eyes.

12. Spell:
Frankie was known for his --------------------------------- which he mostly got from reading.

Great work you are doing!

Spelling 5-23

1. Spell:
Harry was able to--------------------------------his dad to increase his dinner money.

2. Spell:
The doctor asked the patient to do ----------------------- exercise.

3. Spell:
Jude's -- made him dislike Philip because he was not a Catholic.

4. Spell:
It was a--to have Mr. Martins, the head teacher, teach our class.

5. Spell:
George is a lawyer by ---.

6. Spell:
The children's--------------------------------------will start at 10 am.

7. Spell:
Mark's-------------------------of Spanish words is pretty decent.

8. Spell:
Sarah was wearing so much makeup that we did not----------------------------her initially.

9. Spell:
I am pleased with the spelling book and will ------------- it to all my friends.

10. Spell:
The judge decided that the witness's testimony was not----------------to the case.

11. Spell:
Simon called the -------------------- to make a reservation for his sister's party.

12. Spell:
Gemma was teaching Eden a little ------------------------.

Excellent work, kid!

Spelling 5-24

1. Spell:
The beautiful baby girl was such a ----------------------to behold.

2. Spell:
Sharon married a caring --------------------------------------.

3. Spell:
Liam excels in his intellectual ------------------------------.

4. Spell:
The road sign with an exclamation mark warns of ------------------------- on the road.

5. Spell:
Mr. Lucky will-------------------------- the book after writing it.

6. Spell:
The team led the school to -----------------------------in the finals.

7. Spell:
Hakeem is having a hard time --------------------- his career, and his wife does not support him.

8. Spell:
Mrs. Jones will like to----------------------------her means to charity when she dies.

9. Spell:
The cake that Cole made was a complete ----------------.

10. Spell:
The young -------------------------- rolled his sleeves up before taking off.

11. Spell:
Lucas is a complete -------------------------------- like his father.

12. Spell:
--------------------------------, Terry lost his bus pass and had to pay for the ticket.

You are a fantastic kid!

Spelling 5-25

1. Spell:
John does not ----------------------------------- with Joe's schoolwork.

2. Spell:
Magdalene did not want to ---------------------------- the conversation, so she stayed silent.

3. Spell:
Ruben wants to learn a new -------------------------------- during the summer breaks.

4. Spell:
The ----------------------------- center was closed because of the lockdown.

5. Spell:
Antonio ran when he saw the big tree struck by--------------------------.

6. Spell:
David has done a ----------------------------------- job tidying up his room by himself.

7. Spell:
The three boys were ----------------------------, loud, and noisy, so they were removed from the team.

8. Spell:
He relieved his tense ------------------------ with an ointment.

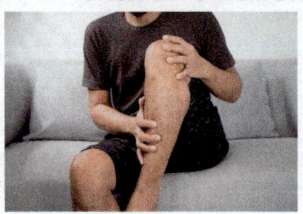

9. Spell:
It is -------------------------------- to write your name on the assessment paper.

10. Spell:
Mr. Samson is Jonathan's new ---------------------- on the block.

11. Spell:
Julie is restless these days and is becoming a ----------- in the dance rehearsals.

12. Spell:
The incident -------------------------- in the class but was not logged in the book.

Good work, kid!

Spelling 5-26

1. Spell:
Harried was quick and -------------------- in her response.

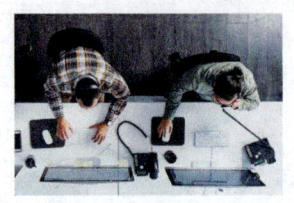

2. Spell:
The pack has ---------------------------------------sweets, enough to cover all the guests.

3. Spell:
The taste of the------------------------------in the cake was delicious.

4. Spell:
The bus driver waited for the--------------------to cross the road.

5. Spell:

The end of the movie did not----------------------------me at all.

6. Spell:

The bus did not --- on time.

7. Spell:

The dogs are -- in size.

8. Spell:

The market----------------------will close her shop at 6.00 pm.

9. Spell:
The holiday travels did ------------------------------Vinnie with new traditions and customs.

10. Spell:
He was not able to----------------------------- his laptop to the internet.

11. Spell:
Courtney did-----------------------------------the teacher's expectations in her spelling.

12. Spell:
I have-- in God; that's why I believe in miracles.

Fantastic work you are doing!

Spelling 5-27

1. Spell:
Mr. Emmanuel bought a new set of furniture to----------- his new flat.

2. Spell:
-------------------------------------- of shouting, why don't we have a calm conversation?

3. Spell:
It was a pleasure to see her ---------------------- wedding.

4. Spell:
Daniel cracked the ------------------------------------joke at the party.

5. Spell:
Bill will not be able to ------------------------------ the family in his house.

6. Spell:
Freya will-----------------------------------Moses to the shopping mall to get his new trainers.

7. Spell:
She is two months pregnant, ------------------------- to the test result.

8. Spell:
The lawyer was slightly------------------------------but did not hurt her feelings.

9. Spell:
Noah is an -- actor who still gets his lines mixed up.

10. Spell:
Although I ---------------------your effort on this project, I cannot give you the promotion.

11. Spell:
Nathan has -------------------------------- the document to the email sent to Jennifer.

12. Spell:
I expect the lawyer will---------------------------------- on time to my lawsuit.

Great! You should be proud of yourself. If, however, you do not feel very confident with some of the words, repeat them repeatedly until you fully understand the meaning and orthography.

Spelling 5-28

1. Spell:
The manager did not----------------------------------him for his work habit but for his clumsiness.

2. Spell:
The teacher sparked my --------------------------- when he was teaching us history.

3. Spell:
The hairdresser gave me a --------------------------- time to come to the saloon.

4. Spell:
Callum was--to finish the spelling book before he got to year 6.

5. Spell:
Riley was -------------------------------------- to finish his reading before he went to sleep.

6. Spell:
Lennie has been doing regular exercise to----------------------- her muscles.

7. Spell:
Looking up words in the -------------------------------- helps you improve your spelling and writing.

8. Spell:
The -- flood demolished most houses in the city's eastern part.

9. Spell:
Chantelle went ahead to ------------------------- the little girl wearing Cinderella attire.

10. Spell:
Keeping the-------------------------------------- clean is essential if we want to sustain life on this planet.

11. Spell:
The old ------------------------------------ in the laboratory was replaced with a new one.

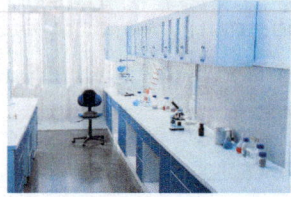

12. Spell:
The science laboratory is well ----------------------- with modern apparatus.

You are becoming a great speller!

Spelling 5-29

1. Spell:
It is safe to park the ----------------------------- in front of Jones's house.

2. Spell:
Riley owns a private --------------------------, and he gets to travel to Greek Islands every summer.

3. Spell:
Her mum introduced the finger --------------------- to help her stop sucking her tomb.

4. Spell:
She is going on --------------------------------for fraud, and the jury will decide if she is guilty or not.

5. Spell:
Julius is now old ---------------------------------- to take the train by himself to school.

6. Spell:
Anton's reasonable ---------------------------------- and pleasant behavior earned my liking.

7. Spell:
The class was so--------------------------------today because we had a new teacher.

8. Spell:
Asif's grandparents left him a considerable -------------------.

9. Spell:
Jude was -------------------------------- of his dad sitting on the sofa.

10. Spell:
His debate did bring a lot of---------------------------to the audience.

11. Spell:
My family enjoys the-------------------------------of living near the leisure center.

12. Spell:
You can call Camron at his --------------------- number after school.

Excellent work, kid!

Spelling 5-30

1. Spell:
Courtney will have to ------------------------- down to look closely at the snail.

2. Spell:
Maddison has booked her train ticket in ------------------ to have a discount.

3. Spell:
Callum saw many ships in the ------------------------------.

4. Spell:
Charlotte drank a cup of orange ---------------------- with her shepherd's pie.

5. Spell:
Any ----------------------------------to escape this prison is futile, the director warns.

6. Spell:
The hotel provided friendly -------------------------to the family on our last visit to Italy.

7. Spell:
Do you-----------------------------------a signature on the application form?

8. Spell:
The youth will be meeting at the ---------------------- park on Saturday.

9. Spell:
Amy chose the ------------------------method to solve the problem.

10. Spell:
The police officers were assigned to ------------------------------ the clubhouse regularly.

11. Spell:
The medicine that the doctor recommended to Anne gave her an------------------ relief.

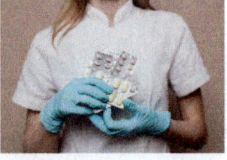

12. Spell:
--------------------------------- after the firefighters entered the room, the fire was put out.

Lovely work, kid!

Spelling 5 -31

1. Spell:
Each ----------------------------- will have a different seat.

2. Spell:
Lainey did not like the--------------------------------of food that was served at the school's canteen.

3. Spell:
Jake won the gold ---------------------------------------in the hundred meters race.

4. Spell:
The --------------------------------- was detailed, precise, and helpful, with clear instructions on what to do.

5. Spell:
The pregnant lady gave her ------------------------------------for a cesarean operation.

6. Spell:
The doctor could not ------------------------------- the treatment because the patient was reacting to it.

7. Spell:
A car, for --------------------------------------, is a type of vehicle.

8. Spell:
The year one child will measure their ------------------------- in class after lunch as part of their lesson.

9. Spell:
Billy raised ----------------------------- for his learning in a noisy class.

10. Spell:
It is a traditional ----------------------------------- to have Christmas dinner with the family.

11. Spell:
The ship is on its way going to the canary ----------------.

12. Spell:
He has ------------------------- the white ball into the net.

Excellent work, kid!

Spelling 5-32

1. Spell:
Always travel with your --------------belt on at all times.

2. Spell:
The sky is the-------------------- if you strive for success.

3. Spell:
The electricity --------------------------- was cut from the building because of the construction work.

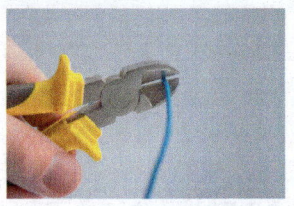

4. Spell:
Mark's boss gave him two weeks -------------------- to find another job before he fired him.

5. Spell:
Daniel is going on a coding --.

6. Spell:
Mariam is -----------------------------of getting the first position, but she cannot be bothered.

7. Spell:
Jude was mistaken for a ------------------------- because he was the last to leave the room.

8. Spell:
Mohamed used a sharp---------------------------to cut the meat.

9. Spell:
Kinsley washed his----------------------------of socks with his hands.

10. Spell:
George told me to clean the --------------------------- after the second attempt.

11. Spell:
Sandra could not go out to play with her friends because she did not ---------------------- her house chore.

12. Spell:
Jamie came -------------------- in the poetry completion.

You are becoming an intelligent speller!

Spelling 5-33

1. Spell:
The class chatted about a ----------------------of things to help their learning.

2. Spell:
Alexis does not feel ------------------------------ in her job.

3. Spell:
Elliot does -------------------------his sister when they are home alone, so she reported him to her dad.

4. Spell:
The old lady said her -------------------------------- to her grandchildren at the hospital.

5. Spell:
The--------------------------------between ten and two is eight.

6. Spell:
Caroline's -------------------------------meal is chicken and chips.

7. Spell:
Debby's mum is always fussy about her ------------------------.

8. Spell:
If you do not have a clear -------------------------------- in life, you end up drifting around.

9. Spell:
Danny got an ---------------------- to attend the seminar.

10. Spell:
There was a fatal ------------------------------ on the main road this morning.

11. Spell:
------------------------------ yourself with only quality people that can help you evolve.

12. Spell:
------------------------------, Gabriel's train was on time.

What Progress! You completed lesson 33 already. You should be proud of yourself!

Spelling 5-34

1. Spell:
Mark reached out to his grandson and tried to ------------------------- his hand but ran away.

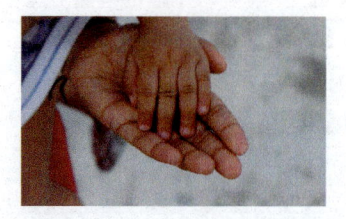

2. Spell:
The -------------------------of his heartbeat is weak.

3. Spell:
Rose had to ------------------------------- her time to look after her sick daughter.

4. Spell:
Jude was in -------------------------- pain after the operation.

5. Spell:
Danny was-----------------------------of Nyla's new piano, so he scratched it.

6. Spell:
Lifeguards ------------------------- many swimmers every summer from drowning.

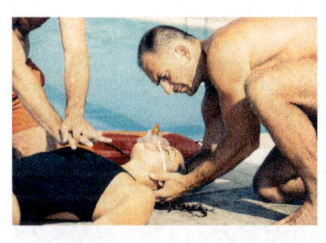

7. Spell:
Abel had the------------------to travel to California to study.

8. Spell:
The members of the --------------------------- are hard-working.

9. Spell:
Matilda loves food, -------------------------- chicken curry.

10. Spell:
Come on, Adam... Don't -----------------------------!
The exam was not that difficult after all.

11. Spell:
Water is a --.

12. Spell:
The construction ---------------------- is booming.

Here we are! Last lesson, and you have reached the end of Spelling 5. Do you feel like you have conquered the vocabulary and spelling field? Great! You should be proud of yourself. However, if you do not feel confident with some words, repeat them repeatedly until you fully understand the meaning and the orthography.

Conclusion

CONGRATULATIONS! You are simply the best!
You arrived at the end of Spelling 5! What an achievement! You have made it, and you should be proud of yourself!
One thing is for sure; I am proud of you!
You should now know how to spell and write down 408 words correctly.

I bet it feels good, right? And it boosts you to continue to the next level.

However, pause for one minute.
Are you confident that you have conquered all 408 words?
Are you sure there aren't a couple of words that need repetition?
Well, you better check it out so that you don't get to have any gaps while proceeding to the next book.
There is no rush.

Spelling 6 will be waiting for you when you are ready.

Please leave a click Review!

I would be incredibly thankful if you could take just 60 seconds to write a brief review on the platform of purchase, even if it's just a few sentences!

Answers

Spelling 5-1

1. Spell: **Opportunity**
2. Spell: **Altogether**
3. Spell: **Although**
4. Spell: **Marvel**
5. Spell: **Groaned**
6. Spell: **Conductor**
7. Spell: **Frequent**
8. Spell: **Describe**
9. Spell: **Angle**
10. Spell: **Slippery**
11. Spell: **Easily**
12. Spell: **Accept**

Spelling 5-2

1. Spell: **Donkey**
2. Spell: **Display**
3. Spell: **Wealth**
4. Spell: **Appetite**
5. Spell: **Transparent**
6. Spell: **Precious**
7. Spell: **Quay**
8. Spell: **Bravery**
9. Spell: **Style**
10. Spell: **Choir**
11. Spell: **Demand**
12. Spell: **Destroy**

Spelling 5-3

1. Spell: **Cemetery**
2. Spell: **Available**
3. Spell: **Average**
4. Spell: **Awkward**
5. Spell: **Bargain**
6. Spell: **Bruise**
7. Spell: **Category**
8. Spell: **Committee**
9. Spell: **Communicate**
10. Spell: **Community**
11. Spell: **Competition**
12. Spell: **Conscience**

Spelling 5-4

1. Spell: **Delicate**
2. Spell: **Ceiling**
3. Spell: **Fragile**
4. Spell: **Fulfill**
5. Spell: **Meddle**
6. Spell: **Venture**
7. Spell: **Relative**
8. Spell: **Decide**
9. Spell: **Ninth**
10. Spell: **Lawn**
11. Spell: **Oval**
12. Spell: **Solid**

Spelling 5-5

1. Spell: **Glitter**
2. Spell: **Collect**
3. Spell: **Cancel**
4. Spell: **Propel**
5. Spell: **Guess**
6. Spell: **Scene**
7. Spell: **Cement**
8. Spell: **Century**
9. Spell: **Compel**
10. Spell: **Judge**
11. Spell: **Annual**
12. Spell: **Local**

Spelling 5-6

1. Spell: **Speedy**
2. Spell: **Angry**
3. Spell: **Fault**
4. Spell: **Forty**
5. Spell: **Grate**
6. Spell: **Ornament**
7. Spell: **Character**
8. Spell: **Situation**
9. Spell: **Tongue**
10. Spell: **Payment**
11. Spell: **Trousers**
12. Spell: **Youth**

Spelling 5-7

1. Spell: **Chemist**
2. Spell: **Student**
3. Spell: **Wriggle**
4. Spell: **Quarrel**
5. Spell: **Crowd**
6. Spell: **Beginning**
7. Spell: **Beauty**
8. Spell: **Imitate**
9. Spell: **Actual**
10. Spell: **Applaud**
11. Spell: **Disappear**
12. Spell: **Balloon**

Spelling 5-8

1. Spell: **Private**
2. Spell: **Appeal**
3. Spell: **Welcome**
4. Spell: **Visitor**
5. Spell: **Mature**
6. Spell: **Achieve**
7. Spell: **Invite**
8. Spell: **Injury**
9. Spell: **Pleasant**
10. Spell: **Survivor**
11. Spell: **Principal**
12. Spell: **Popular**

Spelling 5-9

1. Spell: **Excellent**
2. Spell: **Existence**
3. Spell: **Explanation**
4. Spell: **Familiar**
5. Spell: **Foreign**
6. Spell: **Fifty**
7. Spell: **Frequently**
8. Spell: **Government**
9. Spell: **Guarantee**
10. Spell: **Harass**
11. Spell: **Hindrance**
12. Spell: **Identity**

Spelling 5-10

1. Spell: **Author**
2. Spell: **Design**
3. Spell: **Employ**
4. Spell: **Wound**
5. Spell: **Court**
6. Spell: **Scent**
7. Spell: **Princess**
8. Spell: **Pursue**
9. Spell: **Serial**
10. Spell: **Suburb**
11. Spell: **Solution**
12. Spell: **Decade**

Spelling 5-11

1. Spell: **Wrist**
2. Spell: **Boast**
3. Spell: **Proof**
4. Spell: **Choice**
5. Spell: **Unit**
6. Spell: **Therefore**
7. Spell: **Brooch**
8. Spell: **Generous**
9. Spell: **Visible**
10. Spell: **Usual**
11. Spell: **Royal**
12. Spell: **Eight**

Spelling 5-12

1. Spell: **Broken**
2. Spell: **Circus**
3. Spell: **Pause**
4. Spell: **Noisy**
5. Spell: **Common**
6. Spell: **Plenty**
7. Spell: **Mourn**
8. Spell: **Location**
9. Spell: **Approval**
10. Spell: **Sensible**
11. Spell: **Decision**
12. Spell: **Draught**

Spelling 5-13

1. Spell: **Energy**
2. Spell: **Effort**
3. Spell: **Bacon**
4. Spell: **Protest**
5. Spell: **Silence**
6. Spell: **Breathe**
7. Spell: **Meant**
8. Spell: **Satisfy**
9. Spell: **Falsify**
10. Spell: **Echo**
11. Spell: **Hero**
12. Spell: **Mosquito**

Spelling 5-14

1. Spell: **Advantage**
2. Spell: **Speedily**
3. Spell: **Respect**
4. Spell: **Dangerous**
5. Spell: **Prisoner**
6. Spell: **Irrigate**
7. Spell: **Broadcast**
8. Spell: **Previous**
9. Spell: **Ugly**
10. Spell: **Nephew**
11. Spell: **Department**
12. Spell: **Amaze**

Spelling 5-15

1. Spell: **Magazine**
2. Spell: **Article**
3. Spell: **Habit**
4. Spell: **Uniform**
5. Spell: **Pattern**
6. Spell: **Purpose**
7. Spell: **Regular**
8. Spell: **Scale**
9. Spell: **Salad**
10. Spell: **Accurate**
11. Spell: **Genuine**
12. Spell: **Ability**

Spelling 5-16

1. Spell: **Liberty**
2. Spell: **Achieve**
3. Spell: **Ordinary**
4. Spell: **Motorist**
5. Spell: **Action**
6. Spell: **Brief**
7. Spell: **Error**
8. Spell: **Dining**
9. Spell: **Channel**
10. Spell: **Growth**
11. Spell: **Receive**
12. Spell: **Calf**

Spelling 5-17

1. Spell: **Secretary**
2. Spell: **Shoulder**
3. Spell: **Signature**
4. Spell: **Sincere**
5. Spell: **Sincerely**
6. Spell: **Soldier**
7. Spell: **Stomach**
8. Spell: **Sufficient**
9. Spell: **Suggest**
10. Spell: **Symbol**
11. Spell: **Temperature**
12. Spell: **Thorough**

Spelling 5-18

1. Spell: **Study**
2. Spell: **Foul**
3. Spell: **Except**
4. Spell: **Praise**
5. Spell: **Capital**
6. Spell: **Busiest**
7. Spell: **Umbrella**
8. Spell: **Furniture**
9. Spell: **Score**
10. Spell: **Scare**
11. Spell: **Coarse**
12. Spell: **Niece**

Spelling 5-19

1. Spell: **Drought**
2. Spell: **Nominate**
3. Spell: **Struggle**
4. Spell: **Board**
5. Spell: **Delicious**
6. Spell: **Threaten**
7. Spell: **Careful**
8. Spell: **Quarter**
9. Spell: **Position**
10. Spell: **Amusement**
11. Spell: **Violent**
12. Spell: **Addition**

Spelling 5-20

1. Spell: **Imply**
2. Spell: **Ancient**
3. Spell: **Valued**
4. Spell: **Occupy**
5. Spell: **College**
6. Spell: **Congregate**
7. Spell: **Boundary**
8. Spell: **Bandage**
9. Spell: **Absence**
10. Spell: **Special**
11. Spell: **Chocolate**
12. Spell: **Excitement**

Spelling 5-21

1. Spell: **Cloudy**
2. Spell: **Legible**
3. Spell: **Apparent**
4. Spell: **Application**
5. Spell: **Legal**
6. Spell: **Surface**
7. Spell: **Vein**
8. Spell: **Fiery**
9. Spell: **Introduce**
10. Spell: **Measurement**
11. Spell: **Conversation**
12. Spell: **Engage**

Spelling 5-22

1. Spell: **Mention**
2. Spell: **Argue**
3. Spell: **Debate**
4. Spell: **Biscuit**
5. Spell: **Audible**
6. Spell: **Quantity**
7. Spell: **Either**
8. Spell: **Maternal**
9. Spell: **Electric**
10. Spell: **Shoulder**
11. Spell **Frightened**
12. Spell: **Knowledge**

Spelling 5-23

1. Spell: **Persuade**
2. Spell: **Physical**
3. Spell: **Prejudice**
4. Spell: **Privilege**
5. Spell: **Profession**
6. Spell: **Program**
7. Spell: **Pronunciation**
8. Spell: **Recognize**
9. Spell: **Recommend**
10. Spell: **Relevant**
11. Spell: **Restaurant**
12. Spell: **Rhyme**

Spelling 5-24

1. Spell: **Delight**
2. Spell: **Husband**
3. Spell: **Vigor**
4. Spell: **Danger**
5. Spell: **Publish**
6. Spell: **Victory**
7. Spell: **Through**
8. Spell: **Donate**
9. Spell: **Disaster**
10. Spell: **Aviator**
11. Spell: **Gentleman**
12. Spell: **Unfortunately**

Spelling 5-25

1. Spell: **Interfere**
2. Spell: **Interrupt**
3. Spell: **Language**
4. Spell: **Leisure**
5. Spell: **Lightning**
6. Spell: **Marvelous**
7. Spell: **Mischievous**
8. Spell: **Muscle**
9. Spell: **Necessary**
10. Spell: **Neighbor**
11. Spell: **Nuisance**
12. Spell: **Occurred**

Spelling 5-26

1. Spell: **Prompt**
2. Spell: **Ninety**
3. Spell: **Currant**
4. Spell: **Pedestrian**
5. Spell: **Confuse**
6. Spell: **Arrive**
7. Spell: **Similar**
8. Spell: **Seller**
9. Spell: **Acquaint**
10. Spell: **Connect**
11. Spell: **Exceed**
12. Spell: **Faith**

Spelling 5-27

1. Spell: **Furnish**
2. Spell: **Instead**
3. Spell: **Glorious**
4. Spell: **Funniest**
5. Spell: **Accommodate**
6. Spell: **Accompany**
7. Spell: **According**
8. Spell: **Aggressive**
9. Spell: **Amateur**
10. Spell: **Appreciate**
11. Spell: **Attached**
12. Spell: **Correspond**

Spelling 5-28

1. Spell: **Criticize**
2. Spell: **Curiosity**
3. Spell: **Definite**
4. Spell: **Desperate**
5. Spell: **Determined**
6. Spell: **Develop**
7. Spell: **Dictionary**
8. Spell: **Disastrous**
9. Spell: **Embarrass**
10. Spell: **Environment**
11. Spell: **Equipment**
12. Spell: **Equipped**

Spelling 5-29

1. Spell: **Vehicle**
2. Spell: **Yacht**
3. Spell: **Guard**
4. Spell: **Trial**
5. Spell: **Enough**
6. Spell: **Manner**
7. Spell: **Lively**
8. Spell: **Fortune**
9. Spell: **Conscious**
10. Spell: **Controversy**
11. Spell: **Convenience**
12. Spell: **Direct**

Spelling 5-30

1. Spell: **Crouch**
2. Spell: **Advance**
3. Spell: **Harbor**
4. Spell: **Juice**
5. Spell: **Attempt**
6. Spell: **Service**
7. Spell: **Require**
8. Spell: **Central**
9. Spell: **Easiest**
10. Spell: **Patrol**
11. Spell: **Immediate**
12. Spell: **Immediately**

Spelling 5 -31

1. Spell: **Individual**
2. Spell: **Type**
3. Spell: **Medal**
4. Spell: **Guide**
5. Spell: **Consent**
6. Spell: **Continue**
7. Spell: **Example**
8. Spell: **Height**
9. Spell: **Concern**
10. Spell: **Custom**
11. Spell: **Wharf**
12. Spell: **Thrown**

Spelling 5-32

1. Spell: **Safety**
2. Spell: **Limit**
3. Spell: **Supply**
4. Spell: **Notice**
5. Spell: **Course**
6. Spell: **Capable**
7. Spell: **Thief**
8. Spell: **Knife**
9. Spell: **Pair**
10. Spell: **Mirror**
11. Spell: **Complete**
12. Spell: **Twelfth**

Spelling 5-33

1. Spell: **Variety**
2. Spell: **Secure**
3. Spell: **Dominate**
4. Spell: **Farewell**
5. Spell: **Difference**
6. Spell: **Favorite**
7. Spell: **Appearance**
8. Spell: **Purpose**
9. Spell: **Invitation**
10. Spell: **Accident**
11. Spell: **Surround**
12. Spell: **Fortunately**

Spelling 5-34

1. Spell: **Squeeze**
2. Spell: **Rhythm**
3. Spell: **Sacrifice**
4. Spell: **Enormous**
5. Spell: **Jealous**
6. Spell: **Rescue**
7. Spell: **Opportunity**
8. Spell: **Parliament**
9. Spell: **Especially**
10. Spell: **Exaggerate**
11. Spell: **Liquid**
12. Spell: **Site**

Other Books You'll Love!

1. Spelling one: An Interactive Vocabulary & Spelling Workbook for 5-Year-Olds. *(With Audiobook Lessons)*

2. Spelling Two: An Interactive Vocabulary & Spelling Workbook for 6-Year-Olds. *(With Audiobook Lessons)*

3. Spelling Three: An Interactive Vocabulary & Spelling Workbook for 7-Year-Olds. *(With Audiobook Lessons)*

4. Spelling Four: An Interactive Vocabulary & Spelling Workbook for 8-Year-Olds. *(With Audiobook Lessons)*

5. Spelling Five: An Interactive Vocabulary & Spelling Workbook for 9-Year-Olds. *(With Audiobook Lessons)*

6. Spelling Six: An Interactive Vocabulary & Spelling Workbook for 10 & 11 Years Old. *(With Audiobook Lessons)*

7. Spelling Seven: An Interactive Vocabulary & Spelling Workbook for 12-14 Years-Old. *(With Audiobook Lessons)*

8. **Raising Boys in Today's Digital World:** Proven Positive Parenting Tips for Raising Respectful, Successful, and Confident Boys

9. **Raising Girls in Today's Digital World:** Proven Positive Parenting Tips for Raising Respectful, Successful, and Confident Girls

10. **Raising Kids in Today's Digital World:** Proven Positive Parenting Tips for Raising Respectful, Successful, and Confident Kids

11. **The Child Development and Positive Parenting Master Class 2-in- Bundle:** Proven Methods for Raising Well-Behaved and Intelligent Children, with Accelerated Learning Methods

12. **Parenting Teens in Today's Challenging World 2-in- Bundle:** Proven Methods for Improving Teenager's Behaviour with Positive Parenting and Family Communication

13. **Life Strategies for Teenagers:** Positive Parenting, Tips and Understanding Teens for Better Communication and a Happy Family

14. Parenting Teen Girls in Today's Challenging World: Proven Methods for Improving Teenager's Behaviour with Whole Brain Training

15. Parenting Teen Boys in Today's Challenging World: Proven Methods for Improving Teenager's Behaviour with Whole Brain Training

16. 101 Tips For Helping With Your Child's Learning: Proven Strategies for Accelerated Learning and Raising Smart Children Using Positive Parenting Skills

17. 101 Tips for Child Development: Proven Methods for Raising Children and Improving Kids Behavior with Whole Brain Training

18. Financial Tips to Help Kids: Proven Methods for Teaching Kids Money Management and Financial Responsibility

19. Healthy Habits for Kids: Positive Parenting Tips for Fun Kids Exercises, Healthy Snacks, and Improved Kids Nutrition

20. Mini Habits for Happy Kids: Proven Parenting Tips for Positive Discipline and Improving Kids' Behavior

21. Good Habits for Healthy Kids 2-in- Combo Pack: Proven Positive Parenting Tips for Improving Kid's Fitness and Children's Behavior

22. T Raising Teenagers to Choose Wisely: Keeping your Teen Secure in a Big World

23. Tips for #CollegeLife: Powerful College Advice for Excelling as a College Freshman

24. **The Career Success Formula:** Proven Career Development Advice and Finding Rewarding Employment for Young Adults and College Graduates

25. **The Motivated Young Adult's Guide to Career Success and Adulthood:** Proven Tips for Becoming a Mature Adult, Starting a Rewarding Career, and Finding Life Balance

26. **Bedtime Stories for Kids:** Short Funny Stories and poems Collection for Children and Toddlers

27. **Guide for Boarding School Life**

28. **The Fear of The Lord:** How God's Honour Guarantees Your Peace

Your Free Gift!

As a way of saying thank you for Your purchase, I have included a gift that you can download at TCEC publishing .com

Facebook Community

I invite you to our Facebook community group to visit this link and simply click the join group.

https://www.facebook.com/groups/39768373-37-863

This is a private group where parents, teachers, and carers can learn, share tips, ask questions, and discuss and get valuable content about raising and parenting modern children. It is a very supportive and encouraging group where valuable content, free resources, and exciting discussion about parenting are shared.

You can use this to benefit from social media. You will learn a lot from schoolteachers, experts, counselors, and new and experienced parents, and stay updated with our latest releases.

See you there!

References

[-] https://www.theseus.fi/bitstream/handle/-0024/50239/Anttila_Marianna_Saikkonen_Pinja.pdf

[2 https://www.researchgate.net/publication/28372-084_Early_Reading_Development

[3] https://www2.ed.gov/parents/academic/help/adolescence/adolescence.pdf

[4] http://centerforchildwelfare.org/kb/prprouthome/Helping%20Your%20Children%20Navigate%20Their%20Teenage%20Years.pdf

[5] https://www.childrensmn.org/images/family_resource_pdf/027-2-.pdf

[6] https://educationnorthwest.org/sites/default/files/developing-empathy-in-children-and-youth.pdf

[7] https://www.researchgate.net/publication/263227023_Family_Time_Activities_and_Adolescents'_Emotional_Well-being

[http://www.delmarlearning.com/companions/content/4-80-9224/AdditionalSupport/box-.pdf

[9https://exeter.anglican.org/wp-content/uploads/20-4/-/Listening-to-children-leaflet_NCB.pdf

[-0] https://www.researchgate.net/publication/3-2600262_Creative_Thinking_among_Preschool_Children

Printed in Great Britain
by Amazon